Coping
with Changes

Together We Can: Pandemic

By Shannon Stocker

21st Century
Junior Library

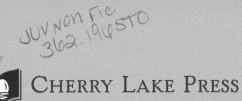

CHERRY LAKE PRESS

Published in the United States of America by Cherry Lake Publishing Group
Ann Arbor, Michigan
www.cherrylakepublishing.com

Reading Adviser: Marla Conn, MS, Ed., Literacy specialist, Read-Ability, Inc.

Photo Credits: © fizkes/Shutterstock.com, cover, 1; © LightField Studios/Shutterstock.com, 4; © Alex Gakos/ Shutterstock.com, 6; © Mantav Jivva/Shutterstock.com, 8; © fizkes/Shutterstock.com, 10; © Monkey Business Images/Shutterstock.com, 12; © Anna Kraynova/Shutterstock.com, 14; © wavebreakmedia/ Shutterstock.com, 16; © VGstockstudio/Shutterstock.com, 18; © miumi/Shutterstock.com, 20

Cherry Lake Press is an imprint of Cherry Lake Publishing Group.

Library of Congress Cataloging-in-Publication Data

Names: Stocker, Shannon, author.
Title: Coping with changes / Shannon Stocker.
Description: Ann Arbor, Michigan : Cherry Lake Publishing, 2021. | Series: Together we can: pandemic | Includes index. | Audience: Grades 2-3 | Summary: "The COVID-19 pandemic introduced many changes into children's lives. Coping with Changes addresses those in an age-appropriate way and gives actionable suggestions to help young readers adapt as we navigate the current outbreak. This includes science content, based on current CDC recommendations, as well as social emotional content to help with personal wellness and development of empathy. All books in the 21st Century Junior Library encourage readers to think critically and creatively, and use their problem-solving skills. Book includes table of contents, sidebars, glossary, index, and author biography"—Provided by publisher.
Identifiers: LCCN 2020039999 (print) | LCCN 2020040000 (ebook) | ISBN 9781534180079 (hardcover) | ISBN 9781534181786 (paperback) | ISBN 9781534181083 (pdf) | ISBN 9781534182790 (ebook)
Subjects: LCSH: COVID-19 (Disease)—Social aspects—Juvenile literature. | Children—Social conditions—Juvenile literature. | Quarantine—Social aspects—Juvenile literature.
Classification: LCC RA644.C67 S74 2021 (print) | LCC RA644.C67 (ebook) | DDC 362.1962/414—dc23
LC record available at https://lccn.loc.gov/2020039999
LC ebook record available at https://lccn.loc.gov/2020040000

Cherry Lake Publishing Group would like to acknowledge the work of the Partnership for 21st Century Learning, a Network of Battelle for Kids. Please visit http://www.battelleforkids.org/networks/p21 for more information.

Printed in the United States of America
Corporate Graphics

CONTENTS

When talking about your feelings, it always helps
to start with the words "I feel."

Dealing with Feelings

Have you ever heard of **coping skills**? Coping skills are things you can do to feel better in sad or scary situations. For example, maybe you talked to a grown-up about your feelings before the first day of school. Talking about your feelings is a coping skill.

Coping skills are especially important when big changes occur in our lives. Changes like that happen during a **pandemic**.

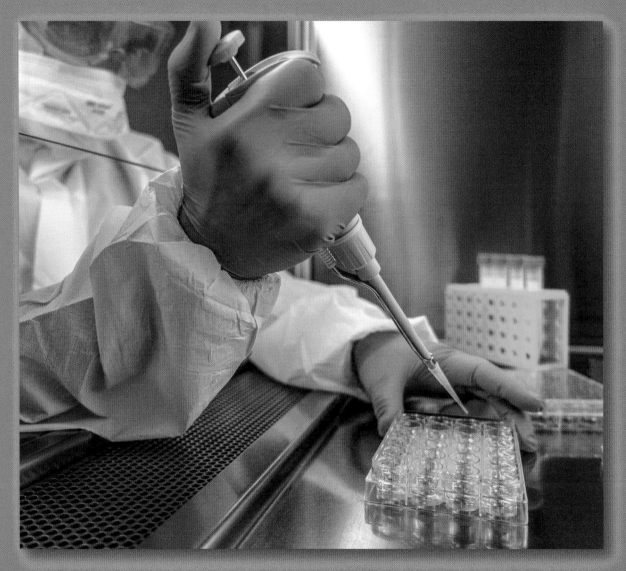

It can take a long time for scientists to develop vaccines.

Pandemics happen when a disease, like the **coronavirus**, infects a large part of the population. During pandemics, people are often asked to **quarantine**, or shelter at home, so the disease is less likely to spread. It can leave everyone feeling confused, sad, and lonely.

But there can be positive sides to quarantine too! Researchers use this time to study the virus and develop vaccines or other treatments that will keep us all safe.

Make a Guess!

What other diseases have researchers studied to keep you healthy? Here's a hint: Think of your vaccinations!

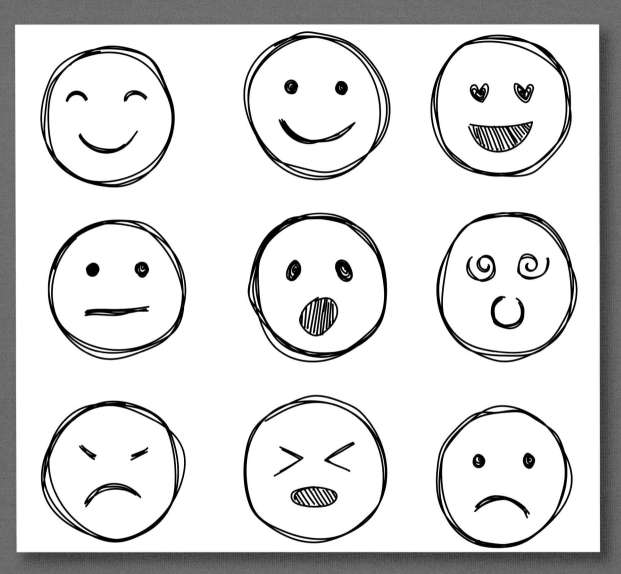

The first step to understanding your feelings is to name them.
What feelings do you see here?

With so much change and uncertainty, how can anyone help but feel a little scared? Well, for one thing, it helps to know that we're all going through this together. You are not alone. Children like you are missing school in the United States, Canada, South America, Europe, Australia, Asia, and Africa. All over the globe, people are learning and adapting together.

Dancing is a great way to get some exercise.
Take a dance break with your family!

Using Our Bodies to Cope

Exercise does more than strengthen your heart, lungs, bones, and muscles. It helps balance your emotional well-being too! Did you know that kids who exercise tend to be happier? When you exercise, your brain releases feel-good chemicals called **endorphins**. These can boost your **self-esteem**, reduce pain, and decrease anxiety and **stress**.

Hikes through the woods can be both educational and fun.
Just be sure to apply bug spray and sunscreen!

Exercise also improves memory and gives you more energy during the day so you sleep better at night. And when you sleep better at night, your brain is more creative the next day. What an amazing coping skill!

Look!

Do you have stairs in your house? How do you think you could use those for exercise?

Try yoga outside! Your body gets vitamin D from the sun.
This keeps your bones, teeth, and muscles healthy and strong.

Exercise doesn't always involve moving quickly. Yoga is a slower exercise with **poses**. It requires paying attention to movement and breathing. It helps you have better balance and posture. And it helps you relax.

Create!

If you were to make up a yoga pose, what would it look like? What would you name it?

Taking breaks from activities is important for staying healthy and positive. Take a break and read a book with a sibling!

Using Our Minds to Cope

Put your hand on your belly. Now, sit up tall and relax your shoulders. Breathe in (count to three). Hold (count to three). Breathe out (count to three). And rest (count to three). Do you feel more relaxed? You should! Deep breathing calms the **nervous system**. It can decrease stress and improve your mood almost immediately. Although you can do it anywhere, it's often easier to practice in a quiet, dark environment.

Deep breathing for as little as 3 minutes a day can increase your ability to handle stressful situations.

Did you know that writing and speaking use different parts of the brain? We know that talking about feelings is important, but so is **journaling** about them. When you're upset or scared, try writing about your feelings in a notebook. It's a great way to explore your emotions and promote calmness in a private way.

Create!

Make a daily journaling jar. List writing prompts on slips of paper—use topics like "flying," "things that make me angry," or "why I love my pet"—and fill your jar with them. Choose a new prompt to journal about every day!

Draw a picture of a tree and write things you're grateful
for on each leaf. This is called a gratitude tree.

Practicing **gratitude** is one of the best coping skills you can use to stay positive during challenging times. It's easy, can help you make friends, and increases **empathy**.

Think about all the things you do that make you feel better every day—remember what you've read about in this book! Find something that makes you happy. Maybe your special coping skill can brighten someone else's day too!

Think!

What kinds of things are you grateful for in your life? Add them to your gratitude tree!

GLOSSARY

coping skills (KOPE-ing SKILZ) actions people take to work through stressful situations

coronavirus (kuh-ROH-nuh-vye-ruhs) a family of viruses that cause a variety of illnesses in people and other mammals

empathy (EM-puh-thee) the ability to understand other people's feelings or "put yourself in their shoes"

endorphins (en-DOR-finz) substances produced by the brain that make people feel happy

gratitude (GRAT-ih-tood) a feeling of being grateful or thankful

journaling (JUR-nuhl-ing) writing, often about feelings or thoughts, in a notebook

nervous system (NUR-vuhs SIS-tuhm) a system in the body that includes the brain, spinal cord, and nerves, and controls all the feelings and actions of the body

pandemic (pan-DEM-ik) an outbreak of a disease that affects a large part of the population

poses (POHZ-iz) certain positions you take and hold as part of yoga

quarantine (KWOR-uhn-teen) to isolate from others

self-esteem (self-ih-STEEM) a feeling of personal pride and respect for yourself

stress (STRES) mental or emotional strain or pressure

FIND OUT MORE

WEBSITES

CDC—Keep Children Healthy During the COVID-19 Outbreak
https://www.cdc.gov/coronavirus/2019-ncov/daily-life-coping/
children.html

Coping Skills for Kids—Deep Breathing Exercises for Kids!
https://copingskillsforkids.com/deep-breathing-exercises-for-kids

DoYouYoga—8 Benefits of Yoga for Kids
https://www.doyou.com/8-benefits-of-yoga-for-kids

Positive Psychology—13 Most Popular Gratitude Exercises and Activities
https://positivepsychology.com/gratitude-exercises

INDEX

ABOUT THE AUTHOR

Shannon Stocker writes picture books, books for young readers, and *Chicken Soup* stories. Her favorite coping skills include writing, music, and outdoor activities with her family. Shannon lives in Louisville, Kentucky, with Greg, Cassidy, Tye, and far too many critters.